T0353165

Oxford

a pocket miscellany

Paul Sullivan

First published 2011

The History Press
The Mill, Brimscombe Port
Stroud, Gloucestershire, GL5 2QG
www.thehistorypress.co.uk

British Library Cataloguing in Publication Data.
A catalogue record for this book is available from the British Library.

ISBN 978 0 7524 6026 0

Typesetting and origination by The History Press
Printed in Great Britain

Coat of Arms

The Oxford ox fording the Thames

*

A black elephant, symbol of seventeenth-century Sir Francis Knollys, High Steward of the City, Lord Lieutenant, and MP

*

A green beaver, symbol of seventeenth-century Henry Norreys of Rycote, Captain of the City Militia, MP

*

A leopard with blue fleur-de-lys, crown and Tudor Rose, granted to Oxford by Queen Elizabeth I after her visit in 1566

*

The motto *Fortis est Veritas*, meaning 'truth is strong'

Contents

Oxford

Pronounced oks-fəd
('ə' sounding like the vowel in *the*)

Means 'ford used by oxen', from the Old English words *oxa* (genitive plural *oxna*) and *ford*. Earlier spellings include Oxnaford and Oxenford.

Grid Reference

Ordnance Survey grid reference: SP 51271 06526

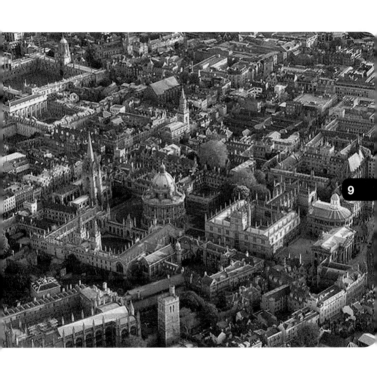

Earliest Appearance on a Map

Oxford first appears on the 1360 Gough Map, named after map and print collector Richard Gough who bought it for half a crown in 1774. It shows 600 towns and cities, 200 rivers and all the main roads, with their length in miles.

Oxford is labelled 'Oxonia' and is depicted by a cluster of four red-roofed buildings, a castle, and one of its famous spires.

The earliest surviving map of the city itself was made in 1578 by Ralph Agas, with several of the city's famous landmarks lining the streets. Copied several times over the succeeding decades, it could still get you from A to B in central Oxford.

Both these maps are kept at the Bodleian Library.

200 km

Street Names

Some of the city's colourful street names, past and present:

Bear Lane – named after The Bear pub, which at various points in its history had a real pub bear. Currently named Alfred Street.

Fish Street – where the fishmongers used to hook their customers. Currently St Aldate's Street.

Gallow's Baulk – changed to the less grim St Margaret's Lane in 1832.

Gropecunt Lane – no prizes for guessing what went on here. Coyly shortened to Grope Lane, then changed to Grove Lane in the fifteenth century; to Magpie Lane in the seventeenth; Grove Street in the nineteenth; it is currently Magpie Lane again.

Logic Lane – named in the seventeenth century after the School of Logicians that was housed there. Formerly Horseman's, and Horsemull Lane.

Londonisshe Street – a bit like London, but not very much… renamed Iffley Road in the mid-nineteenth century.

Mousecatcher's Lane – aka Kattestreete (thirteenth century), Cat Street (eighteenth century), Catherine Street (nineteenth century), and hedging its bets on current maps as Catte Street.

Mr Knapp's Free Board – shrouded in the mystery of history, and redesignated Warneford Lane in 1932.

Rock Hedge – appears to have been a sign-maker's typo when the street sign first went up in 1936. Hastily corrected to Rock Edge a year later.

Slaughter Street – changed to Brewer Street in the eighteenth century, though getting slaughtered doubtless continued.

The Butts – archery practice – 'shooting at butts' – had long been out of favour when this road was renamed Cress Hill Place in 1969.

The Slade – not named after the '70s pop band, sadly.

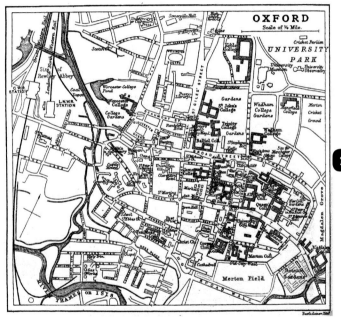

Oxford Ward Snapshots

Barton & Sandhills – seventeenth-century manor, large indoor public swimming pool.

Blackbird Leys – huge council estate, home of the feted Blackbird Leys Choir.

Carfax – based on the original Saxon crossroads at the heart of the city.

Churchill – hospitals, Brookes University and the oasis of Magdalen Woods.

Cowley – synonymous with the Mini (BMW), industrial park and gymnasium.

Cowley Marsh – dense housing, business park, Southfield Golf Course.

Headington – fibreglass shark, old village and Bury Knowle Park.

Headington Hill and Northway – Headington Hill Hall and park.

Hinksey Park – Grandpont Nature Park, outdoor public swimming pool.

Holywell – picturesque old Oxford, Turf Tavern and the Holywell Rooms.

Iffley Fields – suburbia bordered by Thames, woods, meadows and allotments.

Jericho and Osney – defined by river, canal, terraced houses and Bohemian air.

Littlemore – mental health centre, nineteenth-century Anglo-Catholic 'Oxford Movement'.

Lye Valley – wildlife-rich Lye Valley Fen, under threat of development.

Marston – old village, swallowed by the city in 1991, fine twelfth-century church.

North – Victorian Gothic and grand houses predominate.

Northfield Brook – football stadium, bowling and cinema complex.

Quarry and Risinghurst – Morris dancers, nature reserve, C.S. Lewis links.

Rose Hill and Iffley – suburbia, ancient church, Landmark Trust rectory.

St Clement's – includes South Park with great views of the city spires.

St Margaret's – rich Victorian Oxford around Woodstock and Banbury Roads.

St Mary's – internationally flavoured Cowley Road, students, pubs, venues.

Summertown – home of BBC Oxford, shops, and lots of big houses.

Wolvercote – Wolvercote Common and Port Meadow, eighteenth-century paper mill.

Distance From...

Place	Km	Miles
Ayers Rock, Northern Territory	15,077	9,373
Brussels, Belgium	401	249
Centre of the Earth	6,370	3,958
Death Valley	8,169	5,076
Eiffel Tower, Paris	850	528
Frankfurt, Germany	718	446
Guernsey, Channel Islands	157	253
Hong Kong	9,674	6,011
Isle of Man	343	213
Jerusalem	3,690	2,293
The Kremlin, Moscow	2,557	1,589
London Eye	83	52
The Moon (average distance) (NB: varies by 23,000 km due to elliptical orbit)	382,500	237,674
The North Pole	6,761	4,201
Osaka, Japan	9,517	5,914
The Panama Canal	8,414	5,228
Queenstown, SA	9,691	6,022
Reykjavik, Iceland	1,824	1,133
The Sun (NB: varies by 5,000,000 km due to eliptical orbit)	147 to 152 million	91.5 to 94.5 million
The Taj Mahal	6,950	4,319
Ural Mountains (Yekaterinburg)	3,832	2,381
Vatican City	1,506	936
Washington DC	5,812	3,612
Xanthi, Greece	2,304	1,431
Yellowstone National Park	7,371	4,580
Zurich	857	532

Town Twinnings

Leiden, Netherlands, since 1946

Leiden, like Oxford, is criss-crossed by waterways, has the country's oldest university, and is full of students and lecturers on bikes. On 3 October each year, an Oxford deputation joins the citizens of Leiden for a meal of bread and herrings, doled out from the Town Hall. This is called the 'hutspot' and commemorates the end of the Spanish siege of Leiden 1574.

Bonn Germany, since 1947

Bonn Square in Oxford is named in honour of this twinning, which was established just two years after the end of the Second World War. Bonn was the birthplace of Beethoven, and Oxford shares links with the town across all the arts, including music. The cities celebrate their friendship every two years with a week of cross-cultural events.

Leon, Nicaragua, since 1986

The city has South America's oldest university. It is in a very poor country, a situation not assisted by the region's record of volcanic eruptions, hurricanes and tidal waves. Oxford has assisted both financially and practically, raising money for health and education, and welcoming delegations, including Nicaraguan doctors wishing to learn English.

Grenoble, France, since 1989

Grenoble has one of the country's oldest universities, and, like modern Oxford, is at the forefront of scientific and hi-tech research. The cities enjoy sporting links too, Grenoble being the 'Capitol of the Alps', where 50% of the population engage in sport (including activities which are a bit elusive in Oxford, such as skiing and mountain climbing).

Perm, Russia, since 1995

Oxford University and Oxford Brookes University both have links with the parallel establishment in Perm. It is the easternmost city in Europe, 1,450 km (900 miles) east of Moscow, and the greater Perm region, which is linked with the county of Oxfordshire, is the size of England. The two cities get together in everything from politics and education to disability issues and folk music.

Oxford International

Oxford, England, is not alone. The following corners of the world also have Oxfords:

Barbados has one in Saint Peter.

Canada has Oxfords in Ontario and Nova Scotia.

New Zealand has one in Auckland.

The USA has Oxfords all over the place: State of Ohio, Butler County; Massachusetts, Worcester County; Alabama, Calhoun County; State of Mississippi, Lafayette County; Michigan, Oakland County; Connecticut, New Haven County; Pennsylvania, Chester County; New Jersey, Warren County; State of Georgia, Newton County; State of New York, Chenango County; State of Maine, Oxford County; State of Indiana, Benton County; State of Kansas, Sumner County; Maryland, Talbot County; Iowa, Johnson County; State of Wisconsin, Marquette County; State of North Carolina, Granville County.

Jamaica has two Oxfords, in Parish of St Thomas, and Parish of Manchester.

Suriname has one in Coronie.

THE OXFORD COUNTY COURT HOUSE

THE FIRST COURT HOUSE BUILT ON THIS SITE IN 1839 SERVED THE DISTRICT OF BROCK AND LATER THE COUNTY OF OXFORD IT WAS REPLACED IN 1890, BUT THIS COURT HOUSE WAS NOT COMPLETED FOR 3 YEARS. COUNCIL HELD THEIR FIRST MEETING ON DECEMBER 6, 1892. BUILDING PLANS AND FINANCIAL PROBLEMS DELAYED THE CONSTRUCTION. IT IS AN OUTSTANDING EXAMPLE OF LATE VICTORIAN STYLE OF ARCHITECTURE.

WOODSTOCK DISTRICT   MAY 19
CHAMBER OF COMMERCE
AND OXFORD HISTORICAL SOCIETY

Timeline

Death of St Frideswide, whose Abbey church survives at Christchurch College.

St Scholastica's Day 'Town versus Gown' riots result in massacre of students.

The University Botani Gardens open, the oldest in the country.

First evidence of human settlement in Neolithic times.

Oxford Castle founded by Robert D'Oily.

Martyrdom at the stake for Protestants Cranmer, Latimer and Ridley.

City sacked by Vikings.

Gains city status.

4000 BC   735   1009   1071   1355   1542   1555   162

c. 300   912   1018   1249   1478   1545   1602

Roman settlement north of present city.

King Canute crowned king here.

First book printed in Oxford.

Bodleian Library opens, originally a collection of 2,000 books.

First historical mention of Oxford, under King Edward the Elder.

University College founded by friars, beginnings of the modern University.

Osney Abbey destroyed in Henry VIII's Dissolution.

James Gibbs' Radcliffe
Camera building completed.

The Inklings, including
C.S. Lewis and J.R.R.
Tolkien, inaugurated.

University
Museum of Natural
History opens.

Royalist Oxford
falls to Cromwell's
Parliamentarians.

Oxford Brookes
University receives
charter (formerly
the Polytechnic).

Town Hall
opened by the
Prince of Wales.

Oxford Canal
opens to traffic.

1646   1749   1790   1860   1897   1939   1991

1634   1651   1773   1810   1865   1913   1954   2006

James Sadler's
balloon ascent
in Oxford
makes him
Britain's first
aeronaut.

William Morris
begins making
cars in the city.

Former prison
at Oxford Castle,
closed in 1996,
opens as tourist
attraction.

Britain's first
Coffee House
opens in the city.

Poet Matthew
Arnold writes
of 'that city with
her dreaming
spires'.

Oxford University
Press founded.

The Indoor Market
sets up its stalls.

Oxford student Roger
Bannister runs first sub-
four minute mile at Iffley.

23

Seasons

Temperature:
Average temperatures for the city peak at 20.5C (68.9F) in July, with lows of 5.2C (41.4F) in January.

Heatwaves:
The highest temperature on record is 35.1C (95F) in August 1932. The hottest summer was 1976, with fourteen consecutive days of temperatures above 30C. The warmest month on record, with an average of 27.1C (80.8F), was July 2006.

Freezes:
January 1776 was the coldest month on record, with a daytime average of -8C (17.6F) on the 27th. Dr Hornsby, who recorded this, added 'Wine keg froze in study!' The next coldest month was January 1963, averaging -5.8C (21.5F).

There were cold snaps in 2010, with -17C (1.4F) recorded on 10 January, and 28 November ranging between -1C and -8C (17.6F). The deepest snow on record was in February 1888, with 610mm (24in).

Rainfall:
The average annual rainfall in Oxford is 642mm (25in), with October being the wettest month.

Floods:
Flooding was common before drainage improvements in the twentieth century, and flood plains such as Port Meadow often remained submerged all winter.

Bad floods occurred in December 1852, November 1894, June 1903, March 1947, November 1954, December 1979, April 1998 and July 2007.

A witness in 1852 wrote: 'The Isis was amplified to the width of the Christchurch meadows; the Broad Walk had a peep of itself upside down in the glassy mirror; the windings of the Cherwell could only be traced by the trees on its banks... Posts and rails, and hay, and a miscellaneous collection of articles, were swept along by the current, together with the bodies of hapless sheep and pigs.'

24-Hour Timeline

Carfax Quarterboys strike first of ninety-six daily chimes.

Commuters gather on cold railway and bus platforms for London services.

Thousands of students gather at morning lectures.

Twenty-four-hour university libraries make transition from night to day shift.

Choristers arrive at Christchurch Song School for daily term-time practice.

City museums open doors.

0015   0500   0630   0800   0900   1000

0000   0200   0600   0700   0830   0930   1200

Night buses and taxis take over from daytime services and bicycles.

Dawn. Fallow deer stir in Magdalen park as roe deer and muntjac retire.

Breakfast shift at Indoor Market and Cowley Road venues in full swing.

Parks and meadows with al fres lunches ar picnickers

Late-night venues shed last of insomniac revellers.

Morning buses already filling city streets.

Tourists begin to pack main thoroughfares and sightseeing hotspots.

28

Afternoon river cruises share rivers with rowers and punters.

Ghost tours stalk the streets, in season.

Old Tom bell at Christchurch chimes 101 times nightly.

[p]eak time [f]or open-top [t]our buses [d]escribing [O]xford in ten [la]nguages.

Shops close; bus stops crammed with homeward bound shoppers and workers.

Table at Jamie's Italian? You'll have to join long queue on George Street.

Champagne corks pop by riversides for various balls, bashes and birthdays.

1300   **1430**   **1730**   **1900**   **2000**   **2105**   **2300**
1330   **1600**   **1800**   **1930**   **2030**   **2200**

Weekly and summer markets pack away, showering bargains on late shoppers.

Evening theatre and evening cinema shift begins.

Restaurants gently empty as pub and club nightshift takes over.

Tour guides spout University, literature and Morse, according to season.

Early doors: pub fires roar / beer gardens drip sunshine, depending on month.

Live music kicks off somewhere in city, concerts and sessions galore.

How Many Times a Year...

...is the city visited by tourists?
9.3 million

...is the Old Tom bell at Christchurch College
rung in the evening?
36,865

...does Oxford United Football Club play a
home game at Kassam Stadium?
24

...is an Oxford University bursary awarded to a new student?
2,500

...does a single oarsman make a stroke in an
Oxford-Cambridge Boat Race?
600

...is a new Oxford University Press book published?
4,600

...is a crime reported in Oxford?
21,000

...is a swift ringed at the University Museum of Natural History?
100

...is a new book received at the Bodleian Library?
260,000

Oxford Demographics I

How big?
46 sq. km (17.6 sq miles), of which 52% is open space, with 27% Green Belt.

How many people?
2001 census – 134,248.

2008 census – 146,600, consisting of 34,500 aged 0-19; 95,600 aged 20-64;16,500 aged 65+.

This is expected to rise to 164,700 in 2033. Following the general trend in British society, the largest increase in 2033 will be in the number of people aged 65+.

Also mirroring national statistics, 51% of the Oxford population are female, 49% male.

What's the ethnic mix?
Oxford has a rich ethnic mix, the vast majority (82.8%) being from a white British, Irish or other European background. Chinese form the largest non-European group (3%), with large numbers from African, Caribbean, Indian and Pakistani backgrounds.
(See top diagram opposite)

What first languages are spoken?
Statistics from state schools in the city show a huge range of linguistic diversity amongst the 22% who do not speak English as their first language.

What are the religious views?
Not surprisingly in a city famous for Dawkins and Darwinism, there are more atheists and agnostics in Oxford than elsewhere in the county (about a quarter of the population). But theists still outnumber them, with Christianity in first place and Judaism at number two. (See bottom diagram opposite)

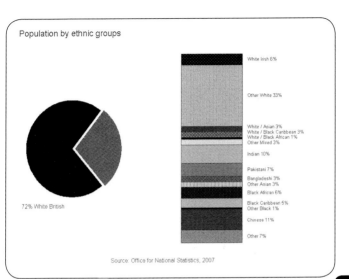

Population by ethnic groups

White Irish 6%

Other White 33%

White / Asian 3%
White / Black Caribbean 3%
White / Black African 1%
Other Mixed 3%

Indian 10%

Pakistani 7%

Bangladeshi 3%
Other Asian 3%

Black African 6%

Black Caribbean 5%
Other Black 1%

Chinese 11%

Other 7%

72% White British

Source: Office for National Statistics, 2007

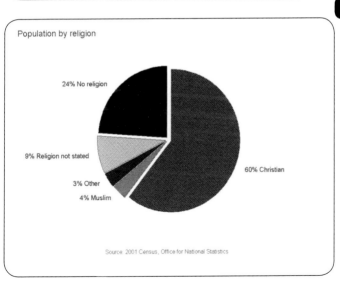

Population by religion

24% No religion

9% Religion not stated

3% Other

4% Muslim

60% Christian

Source: 2001 Census, Office for National Statistics

Oxford Demographics II

How well educated is Oxford? (2009)

As befits a city with two universities, the number of people with qualifications of NVQ4 and above is 45.7%, compared to 32.6% in the south east and just 29.9% in Britain as a whole.

How many students? (2008/9)

26% of the working-age population are students – the highest percentage in the UK.

Oxford University has 23,760 students
Oxford Brookes University has 18,615 students

Who is in work? (2010)

With the high student population, just 69% of the population aged 16-64 are in work (compared to 74.5% in the south east and 70.3% nationwide). Just 6% are unemployed (compared to 6.3% in the south east and 7.9% nationwide).

Ironically, given these figures, there are more jobs than people: 1.13 per person aged 16-64, compared with 0.82 per person in the south east and 0.79 in Great Britain (based on 2008 figures).

What do they earn? (2009)

Average weekly pay is £527 (compared to £514 in the south east, and £490 in the country as a whole).

What's the crime rate?

Incidence of crime varies enormously from ward to ward, but on average there was a 9% reduction in overall crime rates from 2009 to 2010.

Eponymous Oxfords

Several things are called 'Oxford' or 'Oxfords':

Oxford accent – local take on RP and the now extinct 'BBC accent'.

Oxford Blue, Oxford Isis and College White – just some of the cheeses produced by the Oxford Cheese Company. They have a stall at the Indoor Market.

Oxford Clay – fossil-filled clays from the Oxfordian age of the Late Jurassic epoch, around 160 million years old.

Oxford Lamb – sometimes called Oxford John, a dish of seasoned lamb or mutton, sliced thinly.

Oxford Marmalade – Frank Cooper brought this to the world's breakfast tables in 1874, although legend maintains that the original recipe was his wife's invention. Oxford produced the stuff until 1967, when the brand was bought by Premier Foods.

Oxford Ochre – yellow ochre (a naturally occurring iron oxide clay) formerly mined in bulk at Shotover.

Oxford Oolite – coarse-grained limestone, aka 'Oxfordian'.

Oxford Pillowcase – the ones with the 'frame' of material around them, which supposedly stiffens the bag.

Oxford Punch – as in the alcoholic drink, the 'Oxford' has dissolved cow's foot jelly in it. Not in huge demand these days, funnily enough.

Oxford Sauce – an ancient recipe based on Cumberland sauce; and since 2000 'Baron Pouget's Oxford Sauce', bearing little resemblance to the former, has been available.

Oxford Sandy and Black – breed of pig, not unrelated to the following.

Oxford Sausage – recipe open to discussion, but often featuring sage and lemon.

Oxford Shirts – cotton or cotton mix, known as 'Oxford cloth', usually manifesting as sober and smart white, striped, or 'Oxford grey'.

Oxford Shoes – leather, with 'closed lacing' eyelets stitched underneath the top part of the shoe, rather than on top.

FRANK COOPER'S
World famous
ORIGINAL
OXFORD
MARMALADE
Available here!

Famous Oxonian Leaders

Umpteen world leaders have been 'Oxonians' (Oxford University Alumni), including:

British PMs William Gladstone, Herbert Asquith, Clement Attlee, Harold Macmillan, Harold Wilson, Edward Heath, Margaret Thatcher, Tony Blair, David Cameron – and seventeen others!

King Harald V of Norway.

King Abdullah II of Jordan.

John Gordon, Malcolm Fraser, and Bob Hawke, Australian PMs.

Lester B. Pearson and John Turner, Canadian PMs.

Manmohan Singh and Indira Gandhi, Indian PMs.

Liaquat Ali Khan, Huseyn Shaheed Suhrawardy, Zulfigar Ali Bhutto, and Benazir Bhutto, Pakistan MPs.

Norman Washington Manley, Premier of Jamaica.

Eric Williams, first Prime Minister of Trinidad and Tobago.

Alvaro Uribe, former President of Colombia.

Abhisit Vejjajiva, Prime Minister of Thailand.

Bill Clinton is so far the only US President Oxonian.

Quotations from Literature

'And that sweet City with her dreaming spires
She needs not June for beauty's heightening.'
(Matthew Arnold, Thyrsis, 1865)

'Hail, Oxford, hail! Of all that's good and great,
Of all that's fair, the guardian and the seat.'
(Thomas Warton, Triumph of Isis, 1749)

'There are plenty of dogs in the town of Oxford. Montmorency
had eleven fights on the first day, and fourteen on the second,
and evidently thought he had got to heaven.'
(Jerome K. Jerome, Three Men in a Boat, 1889)

'In Oxford City there lived a damsel of the fairest beauty bright
And I did my best endeavour to gain her heart's delight.'
(Anon., Oxford City, eighteenth century)

'The truth is that Oxford is simply a very beautiful city in which it
is convenient to segregate a certain number of the young of the
nation while they are growing up.'
(Evelyn Waugh, Brideshead Revisited, 1945)

'The clever men at Oxford know all that there is to be knowed.
But they none of them know one half as much as intelligent Mr Toad!'
(Kenneth Grahame, The Wind in the Willows, 1908)

'The King, observing with judicious eyes
The state of both his universities,
To Oxford sent a troop of horse, and why?
That learned body wanted loyalty;
To Cambridge books, as very well discerning
How much that loyal body wanted learning.'
**(Joseph Trapp, c. 1715, on George I's donation of a library
to the University of Cambridge)**

'I'm privileg'd to be very impertinent, being an Oxonian.'
(George Farquhar, Sir Harry Wildair, 1701)

'And there's a street in the place – the main street –
that ha'n't another like it in the world.'
(Thomas Hardy, Jude the Obscure, 1898)

'You think they would advertise this place, to let people
know it was on the map.'
**(Felix Adler, Harry Langdon and Charley Rogers, Laurel
and Hardy's A Chump at Oxford, 1940)**

'And I will spend my days in grief, will never laugh nor sing;
There's never a man in Oxenford shall hear my bridle ring.'
(Anon., The Clerk's Two Sons of Oxenford, c. seventeenth century)

Quotations from Fans, Critics and Commentators

'After Christmas they [the Danes] made an incursion away through the Chilterns, and so came to Oxford, and burned down the borough, and made their way back on both sides of the Thames towards their ships.'
(Anglo-Saxon Chronicle, AD 1009, translated by G.N. Garmonsway)

'I can't see who's in the lead but it's either Oxford or Cambridge.'
(John Snagge, commentating during the 1949 Boat Race)

'It is Oxford that has made me insufferable.'
(Max Beerbohm, 1899)

'To the University of Oxford I acknowledge no obligation; and she will as cheerfully renounce me for a son, as I am willing to disclaim her for a mother. I spent fourteen months at Magdalen College: they proved the fourteen months the most idle and unprofitable of my whole life.'
(Edward Gibbon, 1796)

'To call a man an Oxford man is to pay him the highest compliment that can be paid to a human being.'
(William Gladstone, c. 1890)

'I wonder anybody does anything at Oxford but dream and remember, the place is so beautiful. One almost expects the people to sing instead of speaking. It is all like an opera.'
(William Butler Yeats, 1888)

'There is at least one very powerful incentive to learning; I mean the Genius of the place. It is a sort of inspiring Deity, which every youth of quick sensibility and ingenious disposition creates to himself by reflecting that he is placed under those venerable walls, where a Hooker and a Hammond, a Bacon and a Newton, once pursued the same course of science, and from whence they soared to the most elevated heights of literary fame.'
(Samuel Johnson, 1793)

'The real Oxford is a close corporation of jolly, untidy, lazy, good-for-nothing humorous old men, who have been electing their own successors ever since the world began and who intend to go on with it. They'll squeeze under the Revolution or leap over it when the time comes, don't you worry.'
(C.S. Lewis, c. 1950)

'I often think how much easier the world would have been to manage if Herr Hitler and Signor Mussolini had been at Oxford.'
(Edward F. Halifax, viceroy to India and ambassador to U.S., c. 1950)

'Oxford still remains the most beautiful thing in England, and nowhere else are life and art so exquisitely blended, so perfectly made one.'
(Oscar Wilde, 1885)

Famous For...

Places...

The University and its forty-six Colleges and Halls.

The Bodleian Library, to which every new book published in Britain is sent.

The Ashmolean Museum, one of Europe's first, recently expanded.

The Bridge of Sighs, only 100 years old but timeless.

The Radcliffe Camera, iconic jewel of cobbled Radcliffe Square.

Carfax, still marking the original Saxon crossroads of Oxford.

Museum of Natural History, home of Darwin, dinosaurs, swifts and dodos.

Blackwell's, THE bookshop.

People...

Thousands of politicians, academics and artists great and small have passed through Oxford. The list includes:

Nicholas Breakspear, who became Pope Adrian IV.

Robert Dudley, Earl of Leicester, chancellor of the University, and favourite of Elizabeth I.

Dr John Radcliffe, founder of the city's hospitals.

William Morris – both of them: the arts and crafts guru and the car industry giant.

Alice Liddell, escaping to Wonderland with Charles Dodgson (aka Lewis Carroll).

Other writers synonymous with Oxford include **Dr Johnson**, **C.S. Lewis**, **J.R.R. Tolkien**, **Colin Dexter** and **Philip Pullman**.

Other Things...

'**Dreaming spires**' – and some notable domes too.

The Oxford-Cambridge Boat Race.

Messing about on the river with punts, pedaloes, sculls and narrowboats.

Choirs and music, including Haydn's Oxford Symphony .

Vast armies of **Oxford-educated politicians**, scientists, artists and celebrities.

Metriculating processions of gowned and mortar-boarded students.

Infamous For...

Places...

Magdalen Bridge – where revellers risk police and injury to plunge into the shallow Cherwell every May Day.

The New Bodleian – completed 1940, criticised as bland and utilitarian though the Old one was always going to be a hard act to follow.

Blackbird Leys – Oxford estate that used to put Oxford in the headlines for crash-and-burn car theft.

Magpie Lane – former HQ of Oxford's Ladies of the Night.

Pitt Rivers Museum – descendants of the original owners of the shrunken heads exhibit were not impressed.

Rush-hour tailbacks at both ends of the working day make coming and going a pain.

People...

The notorious **Robert Maxwell**, former resident of Headington Hill Hall.

Martyrs **Cranmer, Latimer and Ridley (Protestant) and Campion (Catholic)**, roasted in the city centre.

Jacob Bobart Snr and Jacob Bobart Jnr, famously ugly first keepers of the Botanical Gardens.

University lecturer **William Buckland and his son Frank**, who kept, and ate, freerange menageries.

Firoz Kassam, Oxford United FC Chairman after whom their Kassam Stadium is named, former London slum hotelier, dubbed 'the merchant of misery'.

Charles I and his ill-fated Oxford tenure during the Civil War.

Other Things...

The Bullingdon Club, the University's last redoubt of boozy hedonism.

Evolution versus Creation arguments, ever since Darwin saw the light.

The **giant fibreglass shark** embedded in a suburban Headington roof.

Some of the **highest pub prices** in the country.

'Town versus Gown' conflict, no longer resulting in slaughter but still causing regular unrest and column inches in newspapers.

Former bull-baiting strongholds in Headington and Wheatley.

Stark social contrasts: rich Colleges, deprived estates.

Headlines

Accidental death verdict after elephant encounter
(Jackson's Oxford Journal, 21 September 1872)

'George Cox… met a caravan of wild beasts which had been to St Giles's Fair, and the horse he was driving took fright at an elephant. Cox got off the cart and endeavoured to hold the animal, but he was unable to do so, and was knocked down by the shaft of the cart, and very much injured… It was the [Coroner's] opinion that the wheel of the cart had passed over his body. A verdict of "Accidental death" was returned.'

Churchill at Oxford – A volley of questions
(The Times, 24 February, 1934)

'Mr Winston Churchill, who was the guest of the Oxford University Conservative Association, adopted the method of answering questions rather than making a set speech in the Union Society's hall last night. He was not alarmed by the spread of Fascism in this country 'as a threat to democracy in England'. He was sure that the good sense and long-trained political freedom of the English people and our institutions would enable us to steer a course which would not make it necessary to evoke the assistance of either Black or Red Shirts.'

Delay in building of Nuffield College – effect of
rearmanent drive (The Times, 7 September 1951)

'Work on Nuffield College is to stop temporarily when the block now being built has been completed… [In] view of the rearmament drive, less labour and material will be available. [The] building of Nuffield shall be resumed when ration permits.'

Oxford stands at crossroads – and waits
(Manchester Guardian, 15 July 1955)

'…the fruits of a generation of inactivity and lack of planning have crystallized into a traffic jam… I took the opportunity last week of asking Lord Nuffield if he had any ideas on the solution of the problem he has done so much to create. "I have not the faintest idea", he replied. Then he reflected. "Well, what we really want in Oxford , of course, is more bridges" – and then, as an afterthought, "and more roads going up to them, I suppose." How Oxford wishes it could be as simple as that!'

Letters to Newspapers

Towering over the University
William Lord Archbishop of Canterbury resigns his post as Chancellor of the University, on account of being banged up in the Tower of London during the Civil War. He signed his letter:

'That you may have no miss in the least of me, who (after your prayers heartily desired) now writes himself the last time, Your very loving poor friend and Chancellor, W. Cant.' (Open letter, 25 June 1641)

Unreal Ale
M. Dowson, manager of the Lion Brewery, St Thomas' Street, Oxford assures drinkers that there is no arsenic in Morrells' beer:

'The recent regrettable cases of poisoning show what dangers may be encountered in drinking beer brewed from a cheap form of sugar... I would point out that the safest and most wholesome beer to drink is that brewed from malt and hops alone.' (*Jackson's Oxford Journal*, 29 December 1900)

This library doesn't want books...
'A number of the books added to the Library are not worth permanent preservation in the Bodleian... Sir Thomas Bodley himself discriminated between books. "Sundry books," he said, "are in my opinion not worth the buying for an university... Take no riff-raff books, for such will but prove a discredit to our library..." In short, a "library of deposit" does not mean a book dump.' (C.H. Firth, *The Times*, 22 February 1928)

Trying to kick the hobbit
J.R.R. Tolkien writes from Northmoor Road, Oxford, when critics inform him that *The Hobbit*, though brilliant, is a rip-off of older tales: 'Sir – I need no persuasion: I am as susceptible as a dragon to flattery, and would gladly show off my diamond waistcoat, and even discuss sources, since the Habit (more inquisitive than the Hobbit) has not only professed to admire it, but has also asked where I got it from. But would not that be rather unfair to the research students? To save them trouble is to rob them of any excuse for existing... My story is not consciously based on any other book – save one, and that is unpublished, the *Silmarillion*. (*The Observer*, 20 February 1938)

Famous (Non College) Buildings

Golden Cross, fifteenth-century coaching inn off Cornmarket, redesigned as a shopping arcade. Associations with Shakespeare and Alexander Pope.

St Michael at Northgate, at the bottom of Cornmarket, the oldest surviving building in Oxford, with tower dating from 1040.

Medieval houses, timbered and pleasingly anachronistic on the corner of Ship Street and Cornmarket, currently a mobile phone shop and café.

St Barnabas' Church, Jericho. Designed by Arthur Blomfield, the Italian-style square campanile tower was finished in 1872, Jericho's distinctive variant on the dreaming spire.

Said Business School, part of the University, notable for its glass frontage, late twentieth-century blunt, green spire, and wonderful rooftop amphitheatre, worth seeking out in the summer when performances are taking place.

Bath Place, seventeenth-century time capsule of old houses and cobbles, off Holywell Street.

The Jam Factory, formerly Frank Cooper's Marmalade Factory, at Park End Street. Jars of its products accompanied Scott to the Antarctic; fans include James Bond and the Queen. Sad exterior, lively theatre and arts centre within.

Town Hall, 1893, Gothic Revival edifice on St Aldates. Ornate interior, with decorative plaster and towering organ in the galleried Main Hall. Also note subtle elephants and beavers on the exterior lead pipes, echoing the city coat of arms.

Oxford
Colleges and Halls

University College (full name The Master and Fellows of the College of the Great Hall of the University of Oxford, or 'Univ' for short), High Street, founded 1249. Legend says King Alfred got there even earlier, founding it in 872.

Balliol College, Broad Street, founded 1263. Past members include Nathanael Konopios of Crete, who is alleged to have introduced coffee drinking to Oxford.

Merton College, Merton Street, founded 1264. Has the world's oldest academic library, where books were originally chained to the shelves or kept in locked chests.

St Edmund Hall (aka Teddy Hall), Queen's Lane, founded 1278. Sole survivor of the original Medieval academic Halls, but officially a College since 1957.

Exeter College, Turl Street, founded 1314. Alumni include fantasy authors J.R.R. Tolkien and Philip Pullman.

Oriel College (has also been known as the College of St Mary, and King's College), Oriel Square, 1326. Named after one of the College's original properties, 'la Oriole', which had a large Gothic bay window, an 'oriel'.

The Queen's College (originally The Hall of the Queen's Scholars at Oxford), High Street, founded 1341. Knocked down and rebuilt in the eighteenth-century, famous for its weekly lunchtime organ recitals.

New College (full name New College of St Mary), Holywell Street, founded 1379. The grounds contain a pristine section of the original town walls, and a large mound said to have been raised over a pit of plague victims.

Lincoln College (full name The College of the Blessed Mary and All Saints', Lincoln, in the University of Oxford), Turl Street, 1427. Once a year children gather in the Quad to scramble for hot coins while their elders drink ground ivy ale.

All Souls College (full name College of All Souls of the Faithful Departed), High Street, founded 1438. A £654 loan to King Charles I in the 1640s was not repaid until 1857.

Magdalen College, High Street, founded 1458. Rich in gargoyles and decorative figures, one of which is a mermaid with the face of a girl who worked in the buttery, whose beauty captivated the sculptor.

Brasenose College (aka BNC, full name The King's Hall and College of Brasenose), Radcliffe Square, founded 1509. Named after a nose-shaped 'brazen' (brass) door knocker smuggled to Stamford in the 1330s and returned 550 years later.

Corpus Christi, Merton Street, founded 1517. Graduates include James Oglethorpe, who went on to found the American State of Georgia in 1733.

Christchurch College, St Aldates, founded in 1524 as Cardinal College, refounded 1536 by Henry VIII. Holds the record for producing Prime Ministers – thirteen so far.

Trinity College (full name The College of the Holy and Undivided Trinity), Broad Street, 1554. Charles I took all the College silver during the Civil War to make into coins to pay the army.

St John's College (full name St John Baptist College), St Giles', 1555. The College's Kendrew Quadrangle is the University's most recent feature, opening in 2010.

Jesus College (full name Jesus College in the University of Oxford of Queen Elizabeth's Foundation), Turl Street, founded 1571. Maintains strong links with its spiritual home in Wales.

Wadham College, Parks Road, founded 1610. Associated with gay rights since a former warden fled the city in 1739 after homosexual allegations.

Pembroke College, St Aldates, founded 1624. Dr Samuel Johnson dropped out of it in 1729 due to lack of funds.

Worcester College, Walton Street, founded 1714. Original Medieval cottages on site only survived because eighteenth-century demolition programme ran out of money.

Regent's Park College, Pusey Street, founded 1810 (moving from London's Regent's Park). Its oldest resident is a ninety-year-old tortoise called Emmanuelle.

Mansfield College, Mansfield Road, founded 1886. Originally established to enable religious dissenters to study at Oxford – an odd concept in today's pluralist, secular society.

Keble College, Parks Road, founded 1870. Controversial when first unveiled, with its neo-Gothic 'polychromatic brickwork' design, nicknamed 'Holy Zebra' by detractors.

Hertford College, Catte Street, founded 1874 as a merger of Hart Hall (1282) and Magdalen Hall (1448). Famous for the Bridge of Sighs over New College Lane, linking two parts of the College.

St Stephen's Hall, Marston Street, founded 1876. A training ground for Anglican clergy and other theologians.

Wycliffe Hall, Banbury Road, founded 1877. Unashamedly evangelical Christian establishment, true to its founders.

Lady Margaret Hall, Norham Gardens, 1878. A revolutionary foundation, enabling women to study in Oxford for the first time.

St Anne's College, Woodstock Road, founded 1879 as The Society of Home Students, with full College status in 1952. The original ethos was to allow women to study at Oxford without having to join one of the existing Colleges.

Somerville College, Woodstock Road, founded 1879. Once dubbed 'the blue-stocking college', amongst its many female high achievers were Indira Gandhi, Margaret Thatcher, Esther Rantzen and Iris Murdoch.

St Hugh's College, St Margaret's Road, founded 1886. Youngest member was mathematical genius Ruth Lawrence, who joined in 1983 aged twelve.

Harris Manchester College, Mansfield Road, founded in Oxford in 1889, with College status 1996. Originally located in Manchester, and enjoying stints in York and London before settling here.

St Hilda's College, Cowley Place, founded 1893. Established for women, the first male was not admitted until 2008.

Campion Hall, Brewer Street, founded 1896 by Jesuits. The present Hall was designed in the 'Delhi Order' style by Sir Edwin Lutyens, prime architect of New Delhi.

St Benet's Hall, St Giles', founded 1897. Established so that monks from Ampleforth Abbey (North Yorshire) could take degrees at Oxford

St Peter's College, New Inn Hall Street, founded in 1929, with full College status in 1961. Received London evacuees from Westfield College in the Second World War.

Nuffield College, New Road, founded 1937. Founded by William Morris (Lord Nuffield) of Morris Motors fame.

St Antony's College, Woodstock Road, founded 1953. Established to attract international graduates for the study of international history, politics, philosophy and economics.

Linacre College, St Cross Road, 1962, College status in 1986. Named after Thomas Linacre, one-time physician to Henry VIII, who founded the Royal College of Physicians.

St Catherine's College, Manor Road, founded 1962. Built on a water meadow which later became a rubbish tip, the accumulated rubbish raising the ground above flood level.

St Cross College, St Giles', founded 1965. Set up by the University to soak up the growing number of graduates unable to find room in the existing Colleges.

Wolfson College, Linton Road, founded 1965. Prides itself on being the most egalitarian and liberal of all the Oxford Colleges.

Kellogg College, Banbury Road, founded 1990, College status 1994 Established by the Kellogg Foundation, whose founder, Will Keith Kellogg, invented the cornflake.

Blackfriars Hall, St Giles', founded 1994 by Blackfriars Priory (founded in 1221, refounded 1921). Students study philosophy and theology, with English Literature, British History and Classics.

Green Templeton College, Woodstock Road, 2008, a merger of Green College (est. 1979) and Templeton College (est.1965), centred on the eighteenth century Radcliffe Observatory.

Oxford Museums and Galleries

The Ashmolean Museum of Art and Archaeology. Beaumont Street
Founded in 1683. The UK's oldest museum, covering four millennia of art and history.

The Pitt Rivers Museum, Parks Road
Founded in 1884 by Lt-General Pitt Rivers, to house his collection of archaeology and anthropology and provide a teaching space for those subjects. Eccentric, gloomy, crowded, exciting, unique.

Museum of the History of Science, Broad Street
Housed in the Old Ashmolean building since 1924, tracking the ingenious, uphill struggle of science.

The Museum of Oxford, St Aldates
Born in the 1970s, a concise, non-trivialised sprint through the history of the city from prehistory to car industry.

The Bate Collection of Musical Instruments, St Aldates
The collection was donated by Phillip Bate in 1963. Medieval to modern, chiefly woodwind and brass from the western classical tradition, the instruments' evolution of form and function is a musical fossil record.

Christchurch Picture Gallery, St Aldates
Old Master paintings and drawings, based on the collection of General John Guise, donated in 1765, with ever-changing selections on view.

Bodleian Library, Broad Street

Old academic heart of the University, with free access to the Old Schools Quadrangle, parts of it dating from the fifteenth-century. Exhibition Room and giftshop too.

The University Museum of Natural History, Parks Road

Opened in 1860, this is a treasure house of zoology, geology and palaeontology, marking 150 years of research, debate and education.

Modern Art Oxford, Pembroke Street

Founded 1965, modern and contemporary visual art, exhibitions and events.

Oxford Castle, New Street

On the tourist map since 2006: colourful tours of the former city prison, plus Medieval tower and mound and all manner of events and places to spend your money.

Science Oxford Live, London Place, St Clements (but moving to New Road)

Low-tech hi-tech: inspiring hands-on science exhibits and discovery for children, with good exhibitions and a coffee machine too.

Oxford University Press Museum, Great Clarendon Street (by appointment only)

Books, documents and printing equipment from the Press's long history.

The Story Museum, Pembroke Street

Due to open in 2014, celebrating and showcasing all aspects of storytelling for children.

Flora and Fauna

Fallow deer – a herd has roamed Magdalen College's Grove since 1710. Roe deer and muntjac (a Chinese escapee from Woburn Abbey in the 1900s) can be spotted on the fringes of the city.

Water vole – once synonymous with the Oxford waterways, and immortalized as Ratty in *The Wind in the Willows*, the water vole is now battling mink and extinction.

Red kite – reintroduced to the Chilterns in the 1980s, the kite's return is one of English conservation's great success stories. They can be seen anywhere over the city, although they are commonest on the eastern fringes.

Swift – the summer population at the University Museum of Natural History is the most studied colony in the world. There is a book on the subject, and a nest webcam for off- and on-site viewing.

Green woodpecker – a surprisingly common resident in the city's parks.

Mute swan – all swans belong to the Crown, but the City of Oxford Corporation, and some of the Colleges too, used to have an allowance of birds – 'white game' – in days when swan was a feature of posh dining tables.

Signal (or American) crayfish – introduced in 1975, the crustacean is now everywhere in Oxford's rivers and canals. It is naturally aggressive, and a carrier of crayfish plague, both of which are very bad news for the native white-tailed crayfish.

Oxford ragwort – escaping from the University Botanical gardens in the early 1700s, this native of Sicily found the old walls of Oxford to its liking, and has happily colonised wasteland such as railway sidings.

Oxford weed or Oxford plant, aka ivy-leaved toadflax – a native of Italy that followed the ragwort's example and colonised the city's old stone walls.

Poplar tree – poet Gerard Manley Hopkins wrote an ode to chopped-down poplars on the Thames between Oxford and Binsey. But they grew back quickly, and are still an iconic feature of that stretch of river, the fringes of Port Meadow, and elsewhere.

Parks and Green Spaces

University Parks, Parks Road. 28 acres on the banks of the Cherwell. Highlights include the cricket ground (the only one in the world where you can watch first class games for free); the Genetic garden, established to demonstrate how evolution works; and High Bridge, built as a relief project for the unemployed in the 1920s.

Christchurch Meadow, off St Aldates and Rose Lane. Long-horn cattle, boats on the Cherwell, and ample picnicking opportunities. The well-armed cattle no longer mingle with the public.

Port Meadow, best access from Walton Well Road, Aristotle Lane, and Wolvercote. Medieval water meadow covering 178 hectares, never ploughed, an oasis of birds and commoners' grazing animals, large sections flooded for chunks of the year.

Magdalen Deer Park (The Grove), access from Magdalen College. Free to Oxford residents and Bodleian card holders, small charge for everyone else. Fallow deer and other wildlife in mid-city oasis.

South Park, St Clements. 20 hectares of meadow, used for events throughout the year, alive with picnics, students and sunbathers in the summer.

Headington Hill Hall, London Road. Could sometimes be mistaken for a running track as joggers and dog walkers do the long circuit around the trees. Peaceful parkland of birds and squirrels, with views of the back of Headington Hill Hall and the Oxford Mosque.

Shotover Country Park. Multi-habitat treasure of 117 hectares on the eastern edge of the city, a former royal hunting park, where an Oxford student is said to have killed a wild boar by stuffing a Greek textbook down its throat…

Bury Knowle Park, adjoining a former stately home (currently the threatened Headington Library). Children's play area, tennis courts, and some very pleasing sculpture, including the Story Tree, with echoes of Lewis and Tolkien.

Cutteslowe Park, Harbord Road. Busy in the summer with kids' playground, miniature steam train, aviary, crazy golf and more.

Florence Park, Iffley Road. Bowls, tennis, crazy golf, play area.

Opened in 1934 on land donated by councillor and businessman F.E. Moss, and named in memory of his sister. Venue of the annual Royal Oxfordshire Horticultural Society Flower Show.

Hinksey Park, Abingdon Road. Opened in the 1930s on the site of the Oxford Waterworks. Lakeside walk and fantastic open-air swimming pool. Birds include kingfisher, great crested grebe and cormorant.

C.S. Lewis Community Nature Reserve, off Lewis Close. The flooded claypit and sloping woodland provide a beautiful space in suburban Risinghurst.

…And many, many more in this greenest of cities.

Home-Grown Companies

Oxford Bus Company – a city-wide public transport service, including the iconic Brookes Bus and frequent wi-fi equipped coaches to London.

The Oxford University Press (OUP) – one of the oldest and still one of the world's leading academic publishers.

Blackwells – fantastic bookshop(s) on Broad Street, birthplace of the OUP.

Isis Innovation Limited – technology transfer company owned by the University, rolling out five new companies a year on average.

Mini (BMW) – not strictly speaking home-grown, but the mini continues the long car-making tradition of Cowley, started by the Morris Motor Company in 1910.

Nielsen UK – international market research company, with UK headquarters in Oxford.

Oxford Science Park – hosts 60+ companies, including:

EUSA Pharma – specialty pharmaceuticals for hospitals.

Nominet – one of the largest Internet registries, maintaining the register of .uk sites, and managing over eight million domain names.

The Oxford Ski Company – organises luxury ski chalet holidays in the Alps.

RelayWare – one of the founders of Partner Relationship Management (PRM) software technology.

Human Chain – mobile and wireless telecommunications specialists.

Largest Employer

Oxford University is the city's largest employer. When combined with its publishing wing, Oxford University Press (OUP), it provides work for more than 18,000 people, and boosts the local economy to the sum of £750 million (2009). In addition, the University is one of the world's must-see hotspots – over nine million tourists visit annually, bringing in £590 million.

The University in turn brings jobs back into the melting pot. Oxford and its surrounding county have the highest growth rate of 'high-tech' jobs in the UK, and the bulk of these trace their roots back to the University. Technology transfer company Isis Innovation, for example, has spun out nearly 70 companies since 1997, with a combined value in excess of £2billion, and currently filing an average of one patent application a week.

The University's Said Business School is internationally renowned too and has seen more than 12,000 people on their way to greater things.

Job Sectors

Oxford job sectors

Manufacturing	8,600	8.0%
Construction	2,400	2.2%
Distribution, hotels & restaurants	18,100	16.8%
Transport & communications	3,800	3.5%
Finance, IT, other business activities	20,500	19%
Public admin, education & health	49,600	46%
Other services	4,400	4.1%

Of these, 7,400 (6.9%) are tourism-related jobs
Source: ONS annual business inquiry employee analysis, 2009

Some of the leading players in their field, with employee totals:

Local Government – Oxford City Council: 1,400, including 48 city councillors.
Healthcare – Oxford Radcliffe Hospitals NHS Trust: 10,280 (throughout Oxfordshire).
Motor industry – BMW: 3,700.
Third party logistics/consultancy – Unipart: 4,000.
Education – Oxford Brookes University: 2,500.
Police – Thames Valley Police: 2,000 (throughout Oxfordshire).
Libraries – In 2010 there were more than 110 libraries, providing work for more than 1,000 people. New library service cuts will change this, sadly.
Charities – Oxfam: 750 (throughout Oxfordshire).
Market Research – Nielsen: 700.
Public transport – City of Oxford Motor Services (Oxford Bus Company): 570.
Security software and hardware – Sophos plc: 560.
Publishing – Wiley Blackwell plc: 500.

From http://www.oxfordtimes.co.uk/business/top_100_employers/

Oxford Speciality Jobs

Assistant Curator of the Entomological Collections, Natural History Museum. Duties include feeding and overseeing the welfare of live displays of cockroaches, scorpions, stick insects and bees.

Proctors, Proctors' Office, Oxford University. With one Senior, one Junior and an Assessor, these are the University's mixture of policeman, welfare officer, and chief whip. Proctors are responsible for University discipline, examinations, student support and complaints against the establishment.

Pigeon Pest Control, Oxford City Council, who keep the streets relatively free of the unfortunate bird. Since 1990 it has been an offence to scatter food for pigeons on roads and pavements.

OED Editorial Assistants. Researching and recording historical spelling variations by sifting through everything from Middle English and written regional dialects to international English and web-speak.

Town Crier for the Oxford Antiques and Craft Market, and for other Oxford occasions. Not the official City Town Crier, though: there isn't one. The postholder is also Town Crier for Banbury, Chipping Norton and Daventry, and gets to enter national 'Town Criering' competitions.

Head Coach, Oxford University Boat Club. One of the few coaching jobs to focus on a single event, the Coach's prime concern is to train a winning team for the annual Oxford-Cambridge Boat Race.

Lay Clerks, Christchurch Cathedral. These were established by the College's founder, Henry VIII: postholders, along with Academical Clerks, provide choral music six days a week throughout the year, and the choir gets to record and tour too.

Ghost tour guide, Broad Street. The guide (currently 'Phil Spector') takes tourists on the ectoplasm trails of the city. Other themed trails include the landscape of Colin Dexter's Morse and Lewis.

Deer culler, Magdalen College. Old-fashioned marksman who, in the absence of a predatory wolf pack in the Deer Park, keeps numbers down to manageable levels.

"An inordinate fondness for beetles"

...reply of the British polymath J.B.S. Haldane (1892-1964), when asked what could be inferred about the mind of the Creator from a study of the works of Creation.

Born in Oxford

Richard I, King, Duke, Count and Lionheart, 1157.

Orlando Gibbons, composer, 1583.

P.D. James, (Baroness James of Holland Park), writer, 1920.

E.P. Thompson, historian, 1924.

Patrick Mower, actor, 1940.

Miriam Margolyes, actress, 1941.

Stephen Hawking, physicist, 1942.

Jacqueline du Pres, musician, 1942.

Vivian Stanshall, musician, 1943.

John Sergeant, TV presenter, 1944.

Martin Amis, writer, 1949.

Peter Roebuck, cricketer and commentator, 1956.

Hugh Laurie, actor, 1959.

Toby Jones, actor, 1967.

Tim Henman, tennis player, 1974.

Emma Watson, actress, 1990.

Died in Oxford

Buried at Wolvercote
Kenneth Grahame, writer, 1932.
J.R.R. Tolkien, writer, 1973.
Sir Isaiah Berlin, historian,1997.
Elizabeth Jennings, writer, 2001.
Humphrey Carpenter, broadcaster, writer, 2005.
Sir Edward Maitland Wright, mathematician, 2005.

Buried at Holywell Cemetery
Walter Pater, critic, essayist, mentor of Oscar Wilde, 1894.
Theophilus Carter, the model for Lewis Carroll's 'Mad Hatter', *c*. 1894.
Sir John Stainer, composer, 1901.

Buried at Holy Trinity Churchyard, Headington
William Kimber, Morris dancer, musician, father of the folk revival, 1961.
C.S. Lewis, writer, 1963.

Buried at St John's Chapel
William Laud, seventeeth-century Archbishop of Canterbury, 1645.

Buried at St Mary's, Binsey
Siobhan Dowd, multi-prize winning children's author, 2007.

Blue Plaques: Who, Why, Where?

Sir Isaiah Berlin, 1909-97, historian, philosopher. Headington House.

Jane Burden, 1839-1914, married to William Morris, immortalised in dozens of Pre-Raphaelite paintings. St Helen's Passage.

Nirad Chaudhuri, 1897-1999, writer. 20 Lathbury Road.

Sarah Jane Cooper, 1848-1932, creator of Oxford Marmalade. 83 High Street.

Daniel Evans, 1769-1846, and **Joshua Symm**, 1809-87, designers of many Oxford buildings. 34 St Giles.

Gathorne Robert Girdlestone, 1881-1950, pioneering orthopaedic surgeon. 72-4 Old Road.

Norman Heatley, 1911-2004, biochemist and part of the team that produced penicillin. 12 Oxford Road.

Cecil Jackson-Cole, 1901-79, one of the founders of Oxfam. 17 Broad Street.

C.S. Lewis, 1898-1963, writer and academic, creator of Narnia. The Kilns, Lewis Close.

Sir James Murray, 1837-1915, first editor of the Oxford English Dictionary. 78 Banbury Road.

Paul Nash, 1889-1946, modernist artist. 106 Banbury Road.

Felicia Skene, 1821-99, prison reformer, champion of the poor. 34 St Michael's Street.

Roger Bannister, 1929. The plaque commemorates the first sub-four minute mile. University Sports Ground, Iffley Road.

Henry Taunt, 1842-1922, photographer: the Taunt Collection is an important local history archive. 393 Cowley Road.

J.R.R. Tolkien, scholar and *Lord of the Rings* author. 20 Northmoor Road.

William Turner, 1789-1862, Oxford painter. 16 St John Street.

Anthony à Wood, 1632-95, antiquary, historian. Postmasters' Hall, Merton Street.

OXFORDSHIRE BLUE PLAQUES BOARD

J.R.R. TOLKIEN

Author of
The Lord of the Rings

Lived here
1930 - 1947

OXFORD CIVIC SOCIETY

OXFORDSHIRE BLUE PLAQUES BOARD

HENRY TAUNT
1842 - 1922

Photographer

lived and worked here
at 'Rivera'
1889 - 1922

OXFORD CIVIC SOCIETY

OXFORDSHIRE BLUE PLAQUES BOARD

**CECIL
JACKSON-COLE**
1901 - 1979

Entrepreneur and Philanthropist

Helped establish the first
Oxfam shop and office
here in 1947

OXFORD CIVIC SOCIETY

OXFORDSHIRE BLUE PLAQUES BOARD

C.S. LEWIS
1898-1963

Scholar and Author
lived here
1930-1963

C.S. LEWIS FOUNDATION

Some Colourful Oxford Personalities

From an almost endless list that includes:

Sir Tim Berners-Lee (1955 -), alumnus of Queen's College (he got a First in Physics), invented the World Wide Web. Making it sound easy, he once said: 'I just had to take the hypertext idea and connect it to the Transmission Control Protocol and domain name system ideas and – ta da! – the World Wide Web.'

Revd Dr William Buckland (1784-1856), scientist. Eccentricities included keeping a pet bear; having a table made from coprolites (fossilised poo); eating the preserved heart of King Louis IV; eating as many different animals as possible (zoophagy); and scotching claims of miraculous saintly blood in a church by licking it and declaring, 'I'll tell you what it is. It is bat's urine!'

Bob Hawke (1929 -), University Alumnus and former Prime Minister of Australia. He holds the record for drinking a yard of ale (1.7 litres) at the Turf Tavern: he sank it in eleven seconds. He claims this boosted his political career immensely, winning the hearts and livers of a country with a strong beer culture.

Robert Plot (1640-96), naturalist and first curator of the Ashmolean. He believed that dinosaur bones were the remains of giants; that fossil shellfish were bits of the original seeds of Creation that had missed the sea; and that ammonites were formed from petrified urine.

T.E. Lawrence 'of Arabia'. Practical jokes and adventure coloured his Oxford career. He allegedly herded all the deer from Magdalen Park to the quad at All Soul's. The latter is off limits for undergraduates, and presumably deer as well.

William Archibald Spooner (1844-1940). His tips of the slung include 'The Lord is a shoving leopard…', 'a well-boiled icicle…', and 'You have hissed all my mystery lectures. You have tasted a whole worm. Please leave Oxford on the next town drain.' Sadly, they are probably all apocryphal. The man himself reckoned a reference to 'Kinquering Congs' was his only genuine 'Spoonerism'.

Thom Yorke (1968 -), musician and songwriter of Radiohead fame. Consistently named by critics as one of the most influential rock performers of all time. In 2010 he suggested the imminent collapse of the music industry would be 'no great loss to the world' – much to the chagrin of the music industry.

Criminals

Giles Covington, seaman and petty criminal, was arrested for the murder of a pedlar when another suspect pointed the finger in order to gain a Royal Pardon. He protested his innocence throughout, but was found guilty and hanged at Oxford on 7 March 1791. His corpse was afterwards dissected by medical students, and, in spite of regular campaigns to get his name cleared and his remains buried, his wired bones are still hanging in the Museum of Oxford.

The following is a snapshot of a typical session at the Oxford Assizes, March 1801: '…John Munday for sheep stealing; Thomas Horwood, for horse stealing; Thomas Stokes and John Medcroft, for stealing a fat hog and three loaves of bread; John Honey, Thomas Taylor, Richard Faulklner, and Jeffe Wiggins, for sheep stealing, were capitally convicted, and received sentence of death, all of whom are since reprieved, excepting Jeffe Wiggins who is left for execution. Sarah Russell, for stealing wearing apparel… Edmund Higgins, for a burglary and felony… Anthony Beal, for breaking open the shop of Mr. Hemming… and stealing shoes and curtains, and John Beal for receiving the curtains, knowing them to have been stolen, were sentenced to be transported for seven years… John Benwell, for an attempt to commit an unnatural crime [was] sentenced to one year's imprisonment; the other prisoners were severally acquitted.' (*Jackson's Oxford Journal*)

These harsh sentences stand in contrast to the leniency of an 1852 case involving Elijah Noon of Jericho. Noon was found guilty of killing his wife with a sword, the inflicted wound having festered for several days. Convicted of murder, his crime was softened to manslaughter at the Assize, and Noon was sentenced to a mere two years' hard labour in Oxford Jail.

A popular con trick: '…a labouring man passing through the Parks was informed by a stranger… that he had just found a woman lying in the corn stripped naked, and bound hand and foot… with her nose bloody, and robbed of all her wearing apparel, together with 16s 6d in money, and left the whole night in that deplorable condition… [These two] persons… are detained in the Bridewell of this City as Imposters: The woman having been stripped… by her own consent, and laid in a corn field near this City, in order to excite pity, and thereby raise contributions from the well-disposed, pretending at the same time to have been robbed of her money and clothes the Evening before… the whole was a fraud.' (*Jackson's Oxford Journal*, 14 June 1766)

The body of Harold Matthews, a sixteen-year-old kitchen dogsbody at Wycliffe Hall, was discovered on 6 February 1938. It was on the roof of the Hall, and had been strangled and mutilated. Investigations soon unearthed John Stanley Phillips, a religious zealot studying for Holy Orders. Pressed by officers, he said, 'I had better confess. I am guilty.' He told his prison doctors that the details of the murder had taxed him, and that he did not realise that cutting off Matthews' limbs would kill him. Found guilty but insane, Matthews was imprisoned for life.

Ghosts

Queen Matilda, rival of King Stephen during the twelfth-century civil war, was imprisoned at Oxford Castle, and has haunted it ever since. She was the most frequently spotted spectre in Britain between 2007-9, notching up 32 manifestations as a hooded, misty spectre. All together now: 'How did they know it was Matilda…?'

Mary Blandy, convicted of patricide in 1752, haunts the former prison at the Castle too, sometimes accompanied by other, unidentified ghosts. Disembodied voices and poltergeist activity have also been reported. Shouting and throwing things around in a prison? Whatever next.

The Oxford Playhouse has a resident 'woman in white' ghost, who sometimes floats out to the nearby St Sepulchre's churchyard in Walton Street. She has been jokingly described as an astute critic.

Oxford has the country's only exorcised football ground. In 2001 the Bishop of Oxford was summoned to Kassam Stadium to rid it of a curse that superstitious fans claimed had been planted by a malicious Roma man evicted when the site was earmarked for the stadium. It stands as one of the most colourful excuses for a team's poor performance on the field (thirteen defeats in seventeen games in 2001).

Many University Colleges have resident ghosts, not surprisingly. They include Elizabethan scholar John Crocker, who appears all in yellow at his tomb in the chapel at Exeter College; and Archbishop Laud, who was beheaded in 1645 and buried beneath the altar in the chapel at St John's. The latter's ghost is sometimes seen walking a few inches above the ground, and has even been known to bowl its head across the floor at passers-by.

I Love Oxford Because…

It makes no sense!

…A University with no obvious HQ, consisting of a set of rules and forty-odd Colleges and Halls with their own rules and traditions, not always complementary.

…A library that takes all new books printed in the UK but ran out of places to put them many decades ago and has had to overflow underground, and in 2010 to Swindon.

…A city where graffiti is outlawed on College buildings, unless it is to do with University boat racing.

…A mallard-hunting ceremony at All Souls that involves no mallards and occurs once every 100 years (next due 2101).

…A city named after an oxen ford whose location is disputed.

…Possibly founded by King Alfred in the ninth century, but no firm evidence.

…Conceivably hosted Shakespeare at the Golden Cross inn, where his plays were performed.

…Apparently reclassified the deer of Magdalen Park as vegetables in the Second World War to avoid having them confiscated by the Ministry of Food.

…Definitely the birthplace of Spoonerisms, and yet W.A. Spooner denied saying 90% of the things attributed to him.

I Hate Oxford Because…

It makes no sense!

…Dozens of buildings with doors permanently locked to non-members.

…Libraries where even members can't borrow anything.

…Some of the wealthiest suburbs in England a stone's throw from some of the most deprived.

…Oxford marmalade and Oxford cheese, neither made in Oxford.

…Colleges that own chunks of land many miles away from Oxford.

…Finest Stradivarius violin in the world, safely out of reach of the finest violinists in the world.

…The only Cathedral in the world that doubles as a College chapel.

…World's last stuffed dodo eaten by beetles, only head and feet surviving, none of which are on view (what you see in the Museum of Natural History are casts).

Favourite Scene

Summer: a smattering of people in South Park, looking towards the city skyline.

Least Favourite Scene

Too many cars: heading west, you'll be held hostage at Headington roundabout; heading east, the Botley Road bottleneck doesn't want you to get home.

Folly Bridge Then and Now

Martyrs Memorial Then and Now

Carfax Then and Now

Oxford Eights Then and Now

Fictional Oxford

Some of Oxford's most famous residents never existed:

King Mempricius (aka Membric, Menbriz, Membyr), committed fratricide, ruled as a murderous tyrant, abandoned his family for a life of sodomy, and was eventually eaten by wolves. But he managed to found at Oxford and its University in around 1020 BC – according to the twelfth-century historian Geoffrey of Monmouth (who taught at Oxford).

King Lud, who captured two brawling dragons in Oxford in the first century BC and relocated them to Snowdonia.

Chaucer's Clerk of Oxenford was one of the company in *The Canterbury Tales*:

> 'A Clerk there was of Oxenford also...
> Of studie took he moost cure and moost heede,
> ...And gladly wolde he lerne and gladly teche.'

Tom Brown: the 'Schooldays' novel by Thomas Hughes is more famous than its sequel, *Tom Brown at Oxford*.

Jude Fawley is the downbeat hero of Thomas Hardy's *Jude the Obscure,* where Oxford is called Christminster.

Charles Ryder and Sebastian Flyte are students in Evelyn Waugh's *Brideshead Revisited* and its equally famous screen versions.

Inspector Morse and Sergeant Lewis, created by Oxford author Colin Dexter, brought Oxford scenes to the world on TV, and are the focus of dedicated themed *Morse* trails and related guidebooks.

Sir Leigh Teabing is the academic and foil in Dan Brown's *Da Vinci Cod*

Lyra Silvertongue (aka Lyra Belacqua) is the heroine of several Philip Pullman books, including *Lyra's Oxford*, a parallel-universe version of the city.

The long list of fictional characters who are Oxonians (University Alumni) include James Bond, Captain Hook of *Peter Pan*, Jay Gatsby of *The Great Gatsby*, Fox Mulder of *The X-Files,* Lord Peter Whimsey, Ber Wooster, Rupert Giles of *Buffy the Vampire Slayer*, and Charles Xavier the *X-Men*.

Local Lingo

Batells – college bills.

Bird and Baby – the Eagle and Child pub.

Bod, the – Bodleian.

Bops – college discos.

Broad, the – Broad Street.

Bumping races – dodgems-style races on the narrow river.

Chair – an academic post.

Come up – to newly arrive at the University.

Commoner – an undergraduate without a scholarship.

Crew dates – mixed-sex groups meeting for a formal meal.

Eight – eight-oared rowing boat, used in Eights Week.

Formals – college meals where diners wear formal attire or gowns.

Gated – confined to college as punishment.

Gown – of the University (as opposed to 'Town').

Gaudy – reunion banquet at Colleges.

Great Tom – former monastic bell at Christchurch.

Hearty – a keen sportsman.

High, The – High Street.

Highers – postgraduate degrees.

Hilary – the spring term.

Isis – alternative name for the Thames in Oxford.

Island – the Osney district of Oxford.

Maudlin – how 'Magdalen' is pronounced.

Michealmas – the autumn term.

OED – Oxford English Dictionary.

Other Place, the – Cambridge.

OUP – Oxford University Press.

Oxonian – an Oxford graduate.

Plodge – Porter's Lodge.

Plough – to fail an exam.

Porters – guard-like lodge keepers/postmasters/college security men, etc.

Proctors – a kind of college police force.

Regius Professor – one appointed by the Crown.

Quad – College quadrangles.

Quarry – Headington Quarry district, also the name of a celebrated Morris side.

Rustication – temporarily removed from the University.
Sconce – to demand a forfeit for offence against table etiquette.
Sporting the oak – closing a door to signify 'do not disturb'.
Subfusc – formal dress required for exams.
Trinity – third term of academic year; also the name of a College.
Union Society – the University's famous debating society.
Univ – frequently used name for University College.
Up – the route to Oxford, from anywhere.
Vac – University vacations, e.g. Long.

Customs and Traditions

Shotover egg rolling, Easter.

St George's Day celebrations, dragon and all, Oxford Castle, 23 April.

May Morning: carols at dawn, street partying.

Beating the Bounds and Lincoln College feast, May.

Headington Quarry, Whitsun Morris festivities, May.

Eights Weeks, four day inter-college rowing event, around 1,800 participants, May.

Lord Mayor's Parade, culminating at the Castle, May.

Encaenia Parade, full regalia University ceremony, High Street, June.

St Giles Fair, one of the biggest street fairs in Europe, September.

Round Table Bonfire Night & Funfair, South Park (45th year in 2012), November.

Boar's Head Feast, Queen's College, members only, December.

Restoration Day, Magdalen College, 5 October.

Several other College-specific customs, far too many to list!

Festivals

Dancin' Oxford, annual dance festival, February,
www.dancinoxford.co.uk

International Women's Festival, Feb-March,
www.oxfordwomen.co.uk

Oxfordshire Science Festival, March,
www.oxfordsciencefestival.co.uk

Sunday Times Oxford Literary Festival, March,
www.oxfordliteraryfestival.com

Oxford Jazz Festival, April, www.oxfordjazzfestival.com

Oxford Folk Festival, April, www.oxfordfolkfestival.com

Oxford May Music Festival, April-May, www.oxfordmaymusic.co.uk

Oxford Art Weeks, May, www.artweeks.org

Oxfringe Festival, June, www.oxfringe.com

Headington Festival, June, www.headingtonfestival.com

Jericho Street Fair, June, www.pstalker.com/centre/c_fair.htm

Cowley Road Carnival, July, www.cowleyroadcarnival.co.uk

Oxford City Royal Regatta, August,
www.oxfordcityroyalregatta.co.uk

St Giles Fair, September,
www.headington.org.uk/oxon/stgiles/fair/index.htm

Oxford Open Doors, September, www.oxfordopendoors.org.uk

Ghost Festival, October,
www.oxfordcastleunlocked.co.uk/visiting/ghost-fest.htm

Oxford Beer Festival, October,
www.oxfordcamra.org.uk/festival2010.php

Oxford Lieder Festival, October, www.oxfordlieder.co.uk

Oxford Christmas Market, November,
www.oxfordchristmasmarket.co.uk

Secret Places

The Norman church of St Mary at Iffley: one of the finest carved Norman arch doorways in the world.

Completely hidden, The Turl off Turl Street is one of the city's finest pubs.

The old Mill at Osney Lock Marina, visible from Mill Street; including last melancholy remnant of the once magnificent Osney Abbey.

Old Headington, Old Marston, Headington Quarry – intact, picturesque old villages behind the bland exterior of suburbia.

St Frideswide's Church, nineteenth century, oddly proportioned because the project ran out of money and the tower was never completed.

Kemp Hall, one of the ancient University Halls, present building (c. 1637) functioning as a Thai restaurant in a passage at 130a High Street.

Golden satyrs propping up the lintel in a doorway on Turl Street.

Bulwarks' Lane, cobbles and old gas lamps between New Street and George Street.

The snug Half Moon in St Clements: great live music several nights a week, including a long-standing Irish session on Sundays.

Frescoes, including fifteenth-century scene of unicorn and rabbits over the entrance to Merton College on Merton Street, and St Martin offering a beggar his cloak at Carfax.

Old parish boundary stone in a glass case in Marks & Spencer.

Treacle Well, St Margaret's at Binsey, once a pilgrimage spot for its healing waters, the basis for the treacle well in *Alice in Wonderland*.

University College boathouses: all the college boating clubs used to have grand barges, but these have now disappeared in favour of the more practical boathouse. Several can be seen livening up the banks of the Thames in Oxford.

Oxford's Prehistoric Reptiles

Several dinosaurs and sea reptiles are named after Oxford and its palaeontologists:

Megalosaurus bucklandii – 'Buckland's Great Lizard', the first dinosaur ever described. It was pondered over by scientists in the seventeenth century, and finally named by Christchurch's William Buckland in 1824.

Eustreptospondylus oxoniensis – 'Oxford Well-turned Vertebra'. A mini version of T. Rex uncovered in Summertown, 1871.

Cetiosaurus oxoniensis – 'Oxford Whale Lizard', a 'Brontosaurus' type dinosaur unearthed in 1860, although fragments had been unearthed 150 years earlier.

Camptosaurus prestwichii – 'Prestwich's Flexible Lizard', discovered at Cumnor Hurst in 1879 and named after Oxford's Professor of Geology, this is the earliest, smallest member of the Iguanodon family.

Cryptocleidus oxoniensis – 'Oxford Hidden Clavicle'. Discovered in 1879, this sea-dwelling Pliosaur only lasted 100 years: in 1981 it was declared to be the same animal as Cryptoclidus eurymerus, and struck off the dino-list.

Rhamphorhynchus bucklandi – 'Buckland's Beak-Snout', a small pterosaur (flying reptile) once again carrying the moniker of William Buckland.

Poekilopleuron bucklandii – 'Buckland's Varied Ribs', discovered in 1838 and named after Buckland yet again, it was housed in the Musée de la Faculté des Sciences de Caen, which was bombed in the Second World War. A few casts survive, and it appears to have been a flesh-eating beast similar to Spinosaurus, of *Jurassic Park* fame.

Peloneustes philarchus – 'Power-Loving Mud-Swimmer', Oxford's most recent dinosaur, a sea monster discovered by Museum of Natural History staff in 1994 at a claypit near Yarnton. Species first described in 1869.

Local Sports Teams

The Oxford University Boat Club (OUBC) is famous for its part in the annual Oxford-Cambridge Boat Race. The team has produced Olympic competitors such as rower Matthew Pinsent and cox Colin Moynihan, who is part of the team organising the 2012 Olympic Games. Most of the Colleges have their own clubs too.

Oxford United Football Club, formed 1893, known variously as The Us, Yellows, The Boys from Up the Hill (referring to Headington Hill, the team having been Headington United originally). Bought by the notorious Robert Maxwell in 1982, and later by the controversial Firoz Kassam.

Oxford City Football Club formed in 1882. Known as The City. In 2010 fans were given the chance to own the new pitch, which went on sale for £5 a square yard to raise funds for the side.

Oxford University Cricket Club (OUCC), formed in the eighteenth century, has two teams, the Blues and the Authentics. University Parks has been the home ground since 1881. The annual Varsity match is the oldest First Class fixture in the world, dating from 1827. Famous ex-OUCC players include C.B. Fry, Douglas Jardine, Gubby Alan, Peter May, Colin Cowdrey, Ted Dexter, Mike Brearley, Imran Khan, Abdul Kardar, Mike Atherton and Jamie Dalrymple.

Oxford University Ice Hockey Club, known as Oxford Blues, is one of the oldest in the world. Its arch rival is the parallel Cambridge side.

The Oxford City Stars play in the English Ice Hockey League, formed in 1984 to coincide with the opening of the Oxford Ice Rink.

Oxford University Rugby FC, rugby union side, known as The Blues. Annual 'Varsity' battle against Cambridge at Twickenham.

Oxford Aunt Sally is a local speciality, with a pub league sponsored by Greene King. Players throw batons at a wooden skittle 'doll'. It may be an echo of 'cock throwing', where competitors threw at a live bird. It is said to have been introduced to Oxford and the surrounding county by Royalist soldiers when Charles I set up court here during the Civil War.

Sports Teams Facts and Figures

Oxford University Boat Club – the Oxford-Cambridge Boat Race in April attracts up to 250,000 spectators and millions of TV viewers. First raced in 1829, Cambridge lead the series by 79-75. Oxford won in 2009, Cambridge in 2010, Oxford again in 2011. The Club lost its boat house in a 1999 fire, gutting its archive. A purpose-built boat house was opened in 2004 at Wallingford.

Oxford United FC's record crowd at Kassam Stadium was 12,243 against Leyton Orient in 2002. Biggest win: 9-1 in FA Cup first round against Dorchester Town in 1995. Longest unbeaten league run: 20 matches in 1984. Top league goal scorer: Graham Atkinson, 77. Most capped player: Jim Magilton, 18 games for Northern Ireland.

Oxford City FC – Things seemed to be looking up when Bobby Moore and Harry Redknap managed the team in 1979; but they were relegated that season. Evicted from their home ground in 1988, only returning to league games in 1990.

OUCC – Cricket was being played at the University as early as 1729.

Oxford University Ice Hockey Club played the first recorded ice hockey game in Europe, against Cambridge University in 1885.

The Oxford City Stars won the Division 2 championship in their first season and English League Division 1 in 1990-1, winning twenty-three of a possible twenty-eight games. They have folded and resurrected themselves twice. Dan Prachar of Vancouver is their most celebrated coach.

Oxford Rugby FC was formed in 1869, fifteen months before the Rugby Football Union came into being.

The Oxford & District Aunt Sally Association has been around for seventy years, with games played on Wednesday evenings between May and September. There are up to 120 teams in twelve sections, with up to 1,400 registered players.

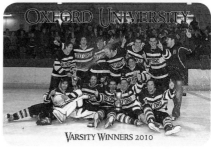

OXFORD UNIVERSITY

VARSITY WINNERS 2010

A-Z

A Alice Liddell: Lewis Carroll's Wonderland muse, raised at Christchurch.

B Boswell's: one of England's oldest department stores, founded in 1738.

C Car industry: from Morris to the modern BMW mini.

D Dead Man's Walk: in Christchurch meadow, old Jewish funeral route.

E Encaenia: honorary degrees procession of Uni dignitaries to Sheldonian.

F Frideswide: Oxford's seventh-century patron saint, founder of priory at Christchurch.

G Gloucester Green: site of market, fairs and bus station, former cattle market.

H Hot-air balloons: Oxford pastime since James Sadler's 1810 ascent.

I Indoor Market: busy, atmospheric eighteenth-century market hall.

J Jericho: Victorian suburb of canals, OUP, cafés and art cinema.

K Keble College barge: last of the University barges, in Museum of Oxford.

L Lion Brewery: former home of Oxford brewer Morrells, now luxury flats.

M Martyrs: X marks the spot on Broad Street; huge memorial dominates St Giles.

N Nuneham Courtenay: site of University Arboretum and the old Carfax Conduit.

O Oxfam: founded 1942 by Quakers, academics and social reformers.

P Printing: one of the city's oldest trades, still going strong.

Q Quad: later Colleges based their quad(rangle)s on the original at New College.

R Radiohead: still the most famous of Oxford's many musical exports.

S Siege of Oxford: three key Civil War Parliamentary victories.

T Tables: College hierarchy sets aside a raised High Table for dining Fellows.

U Universities: Oxford and Oxford Brookes define the character of the city.

V Varsity Match: any sporting contest involving Oxford versus Cambridge.

W Westgate: shopping centre and library, home of Oxfordshire Studies.

X X-ray fluorescence: developed by Oxfordian Henry Moseley, 1916.

Y Young Ambassadors: Uni scheme to inform and inspire local youth.

Z Zuleika Dobson: an *Oxford Love Story,* Max Beerbohm, 1911, his only novel.

Websites

www.oxfordcityguide.com

www.inoxfordmag.co.uk

www.dailyinfo.co.uk

www.ox.ac.uk/colleges

www.oxfordmail.co.uk

en.wikipedia.org/wiki/Oxford

www.oxford.gov.uk

www.chem.ox.ac.uk/oxfordtour

www.headington.org.uk/oxon/index.htm

www.theboatrace.org

www.morsetv.com

www.oup.com.uk

Past and Present – Oxford Castle

From Norman fortress and seventeenth-century Royalist stronghold to city prison and 1990s eyesore, Oxford Castle was reborn in 2006 when it reopened as a tourist attraction.

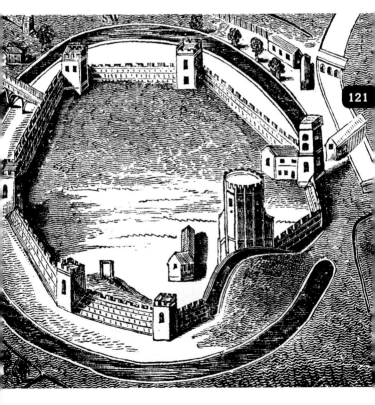

Future Plans

Oxford Brookes University is rebuilding on a massive scale, starting with a new Learning and Teaching Centre, due to open in 2013.

Educational organisation Science Oxford plans to move from its St Clements site to Macclesfield House near Oxford Castle in New Road, with a new centre for science and enterprise, hopefully by 2015.

The Story Museum is due to open in 2014.

The Railway station is due for a redesign, with various plans including a new platform and bridge.

Student flats are being built on the site of Dorset House, a large Victorian building in Headington, controversially demolished in 2009.

The transport and road problems of Oxford have been discussed for decades, but show no sign of reaching a conclusion in the short term.

The Bodleian Library continues to offload new books to its latest extension in Swindon.

TRAIN STATION

GEORGE STREET

NEW ROAD

CITY CENTRE

QUEEN STREET

WESTGATE SHOPPING CENTRE

OXFORD CASTLE

Site of Science Oxford's new development

Things to do in Oxford Checklist

Tour the city in an open-top bus ☐

Check College visiting times and visit at least one ☐

Linger in Radcliffe Square, cobbled heart of the city ☐

Take one of the many themed street tours – ghosts, Morse, Lewis & Tolkien, etc ☐

Climb the twin peaks of Carfax Tower and the University Church of St Mary's on the High ☐

Go shopping in the Indoor Market ☐

Get off the beaten track and discover the timeless cobbled side streets ☐

Take a boat or punt trip, under your own steam or someone else's ☐

Enjoy at least one of the wonderful museums ☐

Visit the city's deer and long-horn cattle in their meadows ☐

Relax with coffee and books at Blackwells ☐

Attend an open-mic session: there is one on somewhere every night of the week ☐

Captions and permissions: where
no credit appears, the image
belongs to the author. Pictures
from Wikimedia Commons, with
Sharealike Licences. Many thanks
to all the photographers involved,
and to Bob Pomfret for his original
cartoons.

Page: